Broadway at Duane St., ca. 1870. (Courtesy of The New-York Historical Society, New York City)

From *Old New York Photo Postcards* © 1976, 1985 by Dover Publications, Inc.

The west side of 7th Ave., with the intersections of 43rd and 44th Sts., 1925, showing the Putnam Building and the Hotel Astor. (Courtesy of Sy Seidman)

From *Old New York Photo Postcards* © 1976, 1985 by Dover Publications, Inc.

Jefferson Market, with the Court House and Detention House, 1926; Greenwich Ave. is at the left, 6th Ave. at the right. (Courtesy of Edward B. Watson)

From *Old New York Photo Postcards* © 1976, 1985 by Dover Publications, Inc.

The Bowery, looking north from Canal St., 1888. (Courtesy of Sy Seidman)

From *Old New York Photo Postcards* © 1976, 1985 by Dover Publications, Inc.

MW00377660

3 (top) The west side of 7th Ave, with the intersections of 43rd and 44th Sts., 1925.

1 (top) The Bowery, looking north from Canal St., 1888.

7 (*top*) An ambulance at Bellevue Hospital, 1st Ave. at 21th St., 1896.
8 (*bottom*) The old Post Office, 1887, with Broadway at the left and Park Row at the right.

6 (*bottom*) In front of the Plaza Hotel, 5th Ave. at 59th St., 1896.

The old Post Office, 1887, with Broadway at the left and Park Row at the right (now southern end of City Hall Park). (Courtesy of Sy Seidman)

An ambulance at Bellevue Hospital, 1st Ave. at 27th St., 1896. (Courtesy of the Museum of the City of New York)

In front of the Plaza Hotel, 5th Ave. at 59th St., 1896. (Courtesy of Sy Seidman)

Cooper Park and the Cooper Union building, 1893, with 4th Ave. in the foreground. (Courtesy of Edward B. Watson)

Manhattan Beach, 1897. (Courtesy of the Museum of the City of New York)

Easter Sunday, 1898, on 5th Ave., looking north from 41st St., with the Croton Reservoir. (Courtesy of the Museum of the City of New York)

Grand Central Station, on 42nd St. at Park Ave., 1887. (Courtesy of Edward B. Watson)

The Fifth Avenue Hotel on Madison Square between 23rd and 24th Sts., 1896. (Courtesy of the Museum of the City of New York)

11 (top) Manhattan Beach, 1897.
12 (bottom) Easter Sunday, 1898, on 5th Ave., looking north from 41st St., with the Croton Reservoir.

9 (top) Grand Central Station, on 42nd St. at Park Ave., 1887.
10 (bottom) The Fifth Avenue Hotel on Madison Square, 1896.

13 *(top)* The *New York Herald* building on Herald Square (at 34th St.), 1900.
16 *(bottom)* Brooklyn trolleys bound for Manhattan, ca. 1897.

15 *(top)* Nassau St., 1908.
14 *(bottom)* Greeley Square, seen from Broadway and 34th St., 1898.

Brooklyn trolleys bound for Manhattan via the Brooklyn Bridge, ca. 1897.

The *New York Herald* building on Herald Square (at 34th St.), 1900, with Broadway at the left and 6th Ave. at the right. (Courtesy of Edward B. Watson)

Greeley Square, seen from Broadway and 34th St., 1898. (Courtesy of the Museum of the City of New York)

Hester St., 1898. (Courtesy of the Museum of the City of New York)

The Times Building, Times Square, 1905.
(Courtesy of Sy Seidman)

Corner of 5th Ave. and 42nd St., with the old
Temple Emanu-El, 1898. (Courtesy of Edward
B. Watson)

Wall St., looking west from Pearl St. toward
Trinity Church on Broadway, 1898. (Courtesy
of Sy Seidman)

Pell St. in Chinatown, 1898. (Courtesy of Sy
Seidman)

19 (top) The Times Building, Times Square, 1905.
20 (bottom) Corner of 5th Ave. and 42nd St., with the old Temple Emanu-El, 1898.

17 (top) Wall St., looking west from Pearl St. toward Trinity Church on Broadway, 1898.
18 (bottom) Pell St. in Chinatown, 1898.

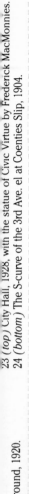

21 *(top)* Broadway, looking north from 46th St., 1900.
22 *(bottom)* Corner of 5th Ave. and 42nd St., with the old Temple Emanu-El in the background, 1920.

23 *(top)* City Hall, 1928, with the statue of Civic Virtue by Frederick MacMonnies.
24 *(bottom)* The S-curve of the 3rd Ave. el at Coenties Slip, 1904.

The S-curve of the 3rd Ave. El at Coenties Slip, 1904. (Courtesy of Edward B. Watson)

City Hall, 1928, with the statue of Civic Virtue by Frederick MacMonnies. (Courtesy of Sy Seidman)

Corner of 5th Ave. and 42nd St., with the old Temple Emanu-El in the background, 1920. (Courtesy of Sy Seidman)

Broadway, looking north from 40th St., 1900. (Courtesy of Sy Seidman)